AIR KISSING ON MARS

AIR KISSING ON MARS

poems by

Kim Dower

Red Hen Press | Pasadena, CA

Air Kissing on Mars
Copyright © 2010 by Kim Dower
All rights reserved

Book layout by Elizabeth Davis
Book design by Mark E. Cull

Dower, Kim.
  Air kissing on Mars: poems / by Kim Dower.—1st ed.
    p. cm.
  ISBN 978-1-59709-166-4
  I. Title.
  PS3604.O9395A75 2010
  811'.6—dc22
                        2010026783

The Annenberg Foundation, the California Arts Council, the James Irvine Foundation, the Los Angeles County Arts Commission, the National Endowment for the Arts, and Sony Pictures partially support Red Hen Press.

First Edition

Published by Red Hen Press
Pasadena, CA
www.redhen.org

Acknowledgements

I am forever grateful to Thomas Lux for introducing me to poetry and irrevocably changing my life so many years ago, and for continuing to be there for my poems. I am grateful as well to Dr. James Randall who directed the extraordinary Creative Writing Department at Emerson College. I toast to his memory. I am grateful to Terry Wolverton for her imaginative, clear, creative, never-ending insights that helped to shape this book, and to the gifted and perceptive poets at Writers at Work for helping to bring clarity to many of the poems in this collection. Thanks, as well, to the poets and teachers at the Palm Beach Poetry Festival and The Sarah Lawrence Summer Writing Seminars for their passionate teachings, endless wisdom, and thoughtful advice and suggestions. I am wildly grateful to my Poetry Angel for keeping desire alive, for feeding me new ways to say old things, and for being there when I was ready. Lastly, I am deeply grateful to the remarkable Kate Gale for believing in me and in these poems, and to Red Hen Press for publishing this collection.

Contents

People Give Me Titles

Cranky in Paradise

How To

For my son, Max

AIR KISSING ON MARS

TRUE STORIES

They took the mailbox away

on Cahuenga and Clinton.
I know because I wasn't feeling right,
decided to take a walk, figure things out,
remember why I love the clouds.
Found my rent check still in my purse,
gave me a goal, a project I could complete.
But when I got to the corner it was gone,
just space in the place where the box had been,
where I've deposited countless bills,
birthday cards, where once I tossed
a sticky half-eaten ice cream dish.
There was no garbage can in sight.
I gave it some serious thought, but now realize
the mess I made: may have destroyed a young girl's
last letter to her grandmother, stained a college
application—what did admissions people think
when it arrived with chocolate sprinkles stuck
to the stamps—worse yet a love letter someone
finally had the guts to send smeared with butterscotch
sauce, possibly obscuring the recipient's address,
sender never knowing it was not received,
when I saw the empty corner
where the mailbox used to be,
granted out of place on that isolated street,
it hit me: the lives I ruined,
the mailman's soiled hands.

She Is Awakened by a Hair

She's awakened by a hair in her mouth.
It's not enough to kill her, no
that would take a locomotive crashing
through her window, a train way off track

thundering through her bedroom,
the moon on its back,
simply a hair
stuck to the roof of her mouth,

her tongue working to pry it loose.
Whose hair is it, anyway?
Is it the same hair she saw
floating in the bowl of vanilla gelato

she ate before bed?
Could it be this hair belonged
to that mechanic she once knew—
they made out on the carousel swan,

kissed til their lips bled—surely
a hair or two had been dislodged,
might have settled inside the cave
of her throat, only to resurface as a wish?

Is it possible the hair was placed
in her mouth by a higher power,
a mysterious donor, to remind her
that dreams are fleeting, even in sleep? No.

No. She realizes this is the same strand
she twisted 'round her tongue
one night when she was young,
sitting straight up in bed,

shadows from her closet
moving in beside her, as she slowly
closed the knot making a promise to herself
she still struggles to forget.

Dying Languages

One language is lost
every two weeks. Researchers travel the world
to interview the last speakers.

Quiet, you can hear what they say:
"She left the parrot in the car,"
"Cut off his leg to make it stop trembling,"

"Keep me safe from myself."
What kinds of languages get lost?
Not ones we speak in Los Angeles

New York or Miami.
A language from a place so hot and humid
words can no longer form in people's mouths.

A language so cruel that people have to cover their ears
so as to not be contaminated.
A language so silly each time a phrase is uttered

people in the streets die laughing.
Now and again men, women, children, goats
faint after overhearing the stupidest thought.

One language will never be lost:
the language of poets struggling to understand
why we die with one word on our lips.

I Love a Man Who Exfoliates

Standing in the aisle searching
for leave-in conditioner,
I see him—tall, giant faced
cornflower blue tee shirt
his wife standing six feet away,
holding the cart, his daughter
squirming inside the plastic bars.
He yells to mother and child,
"I want a good exfoliator, something just for me,
I don't want to worry anyone else will use it."
"Here," she says, pointing to a puffy white loofa
hanging on a string, "this can be yours
we won't touch this."
"Can I use it on my face?"
His giant face must take hours to exfoliate!
What might he be scrubbing off?
Years of sweat worrying
people use his things, eat his sharp cheddar,
housed in its own lock box in the fridge.
He squeezes it to rate its coarseness determine
if it's capable of obliterating his skin cells,
does it have the power to sandpaper
his forehead down to subconscious, I blurt out,
I love a man who exfoliates.

At a Poetry Reading Late Saturday Afternoon

Tired from a long week of caring for others,
working, worrying, walking dogs, feeding
mice, cleaning traps, harvesting crops,
flying planes over deserts, milking cows—
you name it, I'm tired from doing it, the sky is cloudy,
it's warm inside this quiet room, strangers
listening to poems roll out, one after another, lyrical,
lovely, sitting straight in my hard back chair,
my head drops to my chest then snaps backward,
mouth open like my grandfather's at Radio City.
I was seven when he'd take me to see the Rockettes,
"look at those legs," he'd say, then his head would fall,
him snoring, me mesmerized by the line of dancers
glittering across the stage, one long leg lifting after
another. Now in this silent room, the poet reads her
best words, best order, and I'm seven again
when the tonsil doctor put the mask over my mouth,
"count backwards," he said, his fist opening, the foam
bunnies jumping out of his hand, and I was out.
Was it the ether or the whispers of my mother and aunt
that lulled me into a sleep my bones can still remember?
It's so warm in here, so cloudy outside,
and the mice will soon be hungry.

Even in a Dream

Ray Ronci tried to murder me came after me
with a gun I haven't seen him for 30 years
we parted friends but there he was
telling me he was going to kill me drove over
in a Honda with two friends all pale him
so serious I escaped but he came back later his
small black gun covered by tissue
like that would hide it I saw it put my hand
over the hole like that would stop the bullet
like I could stop the days or the leaves from
slipping down the drain pipe falling as fast as
Ray Ronci's hair I could see even with his gun
even in a dream that he'd lost hair
did he see my eyes were not as clear
as they once were it was Saturday when I had the dream
two more days had fallen he didn't shoot me
but his beard was ashen as he took me to my bed
where we lay together in silence
the phone kept ringing

Birth

She can feel the bulk of him:
a three story home parked
under her rib cage.

She can feel them reach
inside her guts
to pull him out,

no pain, just numb tugging,
wet cries from inside
where he lived for nine months,

her tiny kangaroo
waiting like a wish
struggling to come true.

She feels him stretching out,
one last kick to connect them.
She will miss his breathing

into her dreams.
Will he miss her food
invading his?

She tries to picture life
after birth, after they take him
from her body,

her second heart
delivered into heavy arms,
paralyzed by the block

they shot into her spine.
At first, all she sees
are his long fingers,

nails razor-sharp tissue paper
she runs across her lips
tasting the salt of life.

Geography Matters

Taking car service from Delray to Miami International—
60 plus miles, Route 95 past palm trees, junkers, swingsets
'gators giddy with humidity—and I have a driver
who likes to talk. Fingers too chubby for a ring,
his massive back dents the leather, eyeglasses
from the '70s. His accent familiar, maybe Russian,
he points things out, headlines each statement:
let me make you an example.
Turns out he's from Yugoslavia, *where* he says *people*
are better looking, they look better when they come from Eastern
Europe or from the Islands, because it's when people mix
that makes them more beautiful. Let me make you an example,
back home I taught Geography, was well respected,
didn't drive a car all day, though don't give me wrong, I like the people
they sometimes become friends, they like to listen
back home Geography matters here no one cares.
"I care," I tell him, lying, trying to change the conversation.
I tell him I wonder why it takes an hour less
to fly from L.A. to Miami than from Miami to L.A.,
but that only excites him, makes him make another example,
he tells me it's quicker going east because of the earth's rotation,
it's Geography, that's why I know, that's why
I could make you that example, that's why I can tell you why
the clouds move faster in the Florida sky,
why I can't work at the rent-a-car because I need to be outside
even driving all day, and he takes out a pad colored markers,
blocks, wood, pipe cleaners, match sticks, makes me many
examples: a mockingbird wandering the roof, an orange blossom

floating down a creek, a sketch of himself wading through a swamp,
hands me a map of Croatia, grains of white sand slipping
into the creases of the seats.

Visiting Janice

Their pantry has it all:
Sumatra ground, Droste Cacao,
Red Zinger, cereal stale from salt air,
crackers, nuts, sealed with fancy clips,
nutmeg, cat food, no forgotten chips.
Spooked by the wind, Percy, Hello Kitty, Coby
tap to get in, charm us for treats, graze around
on different couches, backs arched for petting.
I love it here:
guest room just so,
ocean across the street pulling me out of bed,
outside shower smelling of flowers and wood,
my face wet against the cool Long Island air.
In the evening their son, tall almost a man,
hangs out with us in the kitchen
Martin, her husband cooks, Janice plays her secret
computer game. We talk to the son about basketball,
books he should read.
We talk to each other about The Who concert,
how Roger Daltry looks so short,
how Janice's hair used to be just like his,
how we hope tomorrow will be
another perfect beach day.
Janice and I, best friends since pajamas with feet;
we played handball instead of class,
foraged for pretzels and chocolate,
greased each other's backs.
Janice on the Atlantic, me out in L.A.,
the screech of the subway we rode to school

embedded in our brains like metal pins.
We are like two atoms shared in a crystal,
our electrons forever sparking one to the other.
We hold hands without ever touching.
Hers is the face I see
when I can't feel my own.
We are sisters without blood
to spoil it.

Dressing Room

She was 14
Summer place
Sand even in town
At John & Anne's
Where there was always
A new flavor to taste
Mango burst her fave
That was the year she wore
The yellow bikini
Everyone was nice
The year her skin was so tan
Her mother worried
Her mother whose mouth broke out
In blisters from the sun
She wore ointment on her lips
Had to stay under the umbrella
While her daughter wandered
The long stretch of beach

She was 14
He was not
Sand even in town
At the bathing suit shop
Where there was always
Something new to try on
She'd seen him on a bike
He turned to look
When she took off her dress
To try on the bikini

He was outside the door
She didn't close it
Let him see her lift it up
Over her brown shoulders
Let him have his look
Her first one
Her mother was under the umbrella
While her daughter wandered
The long stretch of beach

If My Father Were Alive

If my father were alive
he'd be in his recliner sipping scotch
"it's a line drive out to left field"

blasting out the window of his Hollywood
pad, his parakeet yelling with the tv.
If my father were alive

he'd visit on an early fall Sunday
tell me our son is beautiful,
ask why we don't grow vegetables

when we have such a great backyard,
remind me he still had the sunglasses
he wore in cadet school,

he'd be talking about the future
even though he didn't have one.
If my father were alive he'd be telling jokes

to strangers in a Glendale dive.
If my father were alive
he'd be scraping ice-cream

from the bottom of the container,
chocolate sticking to his thick knuckles,
while he slow cooked corn beef,

dinner he invited us to share,
the meal we never got to eat
because his heart gave out swinging

his seven-iron on the Griffith Park course.
If my father were alive
heaven would be calm,

the woman in the apartment next door
would still be dressing up, her fuchsia prints
shrieking into the night.

The Couple Next Door

The couple next door reads all day long.
I can see them from our adjoining hotel patios
high above the sea.

The couple next door sits
at a round white plastic table on hard chairs,
their books touching as they

turn their pages at the same time.
I listen for any sounds they might make:
soft cough, sigh of joy,

I hear nothing except for southbound traffic
on Pacific Coast Highway, distant
waves, morning sounds of housekeepers

cleaning the grounds below our deck.
The man's book looks fat; I see him
thick glasses brand new cap

staring intently into the page.
I never see him smile so I know the book is not funny.
I never see him shake his head so I know the book does not

confuse him, but he suddenly lifts his head
looks out at the ocean, puts his hand over his mouth.
The woman looks content like her book understands her:

it's about something she knows too well—
bringing up children, watching them grow,
saying goodbye.

I brought books too but prefer watching them:
wonder how they arrived at this place
where reading in silence carries them through the day.

The Ant in the Window

I'm walking down Vermont Avenue
attracted by the window,
odd engagement rings no one will buy,

tarnished gold pinky ring
for someone's girlfriend?
the pendant screeching with impossible stones.

Then I see it, one busy ant
racing between diamonds and rubies
STERLING SILVER 35% OFF

YES *we have it . . .*
one black ant climbing over the giant pearl
negotiating its way around the elegant tennis bracelet

stuck in the beveled engraving
WE WILL PAY THE SALES TAX
ON ANY PURCHASE OF GOLD

The ant stops short in front of the sign
like it's interested to know about sales tax,
starts going faster now rushing in a frenzy

circling sapphire earrings like a glitter addict.
As the ant disappears
under a broach the size

of your grandmother's breasts,
I see the necklace of my dreams
35% off.

"They discontinued carrots,"

said the man at Subway when I ordered
my sandwich, *"they are useless filler,*
no substance, no one needs them."
This got me thinking.
Is it possible that carrots really are useless,
even organic ones?
Such a sturdy, festive vegetable,
uninhibitedly orange, *useless?*
Carrots: enemies of peas, slaves
to dipping, I had to know everything,
so I consulted The World Carrot Museum
where I was allowed to "Ask Mr. Carrot" any question,
touch a virtual carrot, sign the guest book, find out
if baby carrots feel emotion, explore carrots in fine art,
carrots through history, vote if carrots taste better
raw or cooked, (this has been hotly debated),
learn about wild carrots, gangs of carrots,
carrots without walls, marching carrot bands,
The Erotic Carrot Film Festival, neglected carrots,
empty nest carrots. Imagine what I felt
after discovering the truth. I had no choice
but to return to Subway, confront him,
challenge him to reconsider,
because if they really discontinued carrots
I, for one, will surround myself
with bunches, swallow them like swords,
carrot juice dripping down my chin,
while I pray for their reinstatement,
careful not to choke on this very sad day.

My Dogs

My dogs follow me
room to room
hoping I'll stay put.
They have nowhere they *need* to be,
free agents, dogs take work wherever they get it.

They think *why can't she sit in one place?*
I pace from kitchen to bath to bed.
They travel tightly by my feet—a couple
of cartoon characters ready to fall
through a hole in the floor.

Scuffling, second-guessing my next stop,
I settle in a chair ankle deep in their itchy fur.
This is it!! They think, *at last she's sitting,
we are safe, we are home!*
But as I get up, the grunt they release shakes the house.

The world they thought they finally understood
once again has changed.
Nothing left for them but to follow me endlessly
into the far away kingdom
of the next room.

Different Mothers

I've read about the ones who garden,
teach their daughters to cut a rose
just above the thorns—so a fresh bud will pop up
like toast in time for breakfast.

These different mothers show their daughters
how to plant tomato seeds in the damp earth,
tingle when the first green fruit appears,
and when they explode into deep red

pick them off the vine, slice them
in their sunny kitchens. These are mothers
whose daughters learn through smells
of lakes, weeds, pastry dough,

have memories of lightning bugs in jars
mothers have poked holes into.
These are different mothers.
I am not one. My mother

didn't know about soil or earth worms.
City mothers, we know about bus routes, restaurants,
Broadway, the people on the eighth floor.
Mine taught me to accessorize, bring the ideal

hostess gift, have my keys in hand
when I enter the building. I have no daughter,
but my son can look anyone in the eye, tell them
what he's thinking. We eat tomatoes

from the grocery. Our roses are store bought.
Different mothers sound better
I think about what might have been:
calling to the birds, naming the stars,

fingers locked together while hiking
on hidden trails, cleaning homegrown mint
before placing it in tea before bed.
I'll flag a cab instead.

Room Service English Muffins

If you've ever had one you know what I'm saying:
soggy with steam, too much butter soaking into the crevices.
At first you're mad—you told them *butter on the side*—
but then you're grateful to have it. Day after day
you eat it dry, now away, alone on business
in your overheated hotel room,
you're grateful for the butter, indebted to strangers
wearing hair nets in a distant kitchen for slathering your muffins,
tucking them into a cloth napkin, placed in a mesh basket,
variety of colorful jams for you to choose.
It's enough joy just to take that first bite, if you're lucky
it's still warm even after the long elevator ride.
If you're lucky there's a yellow single stem rose in a bud vase,
shiny silverware poking out of the starched white napkin.
Why give me a fork, you think? You ordered coffee and a muffin,
why complicate it with a fork? And then you spot the tiny
salt & pepper shakers in the shadow of the napkin, and you wonder,
does anyone, no matter how troubled, put salt & pepper
on their English Muffins? Maybe.
Maybe when they're far from home.

She no longer fears bugs

She no longer fears bugs.
She gets that they're part of life.
She waits for a fly to grab
in mid air, shake in her hand, tape
to her "to do" list.

She no longer fears bugs.
She likes to walk into dark rooms
feel the crunch of roaches
under her boots, watch their shadows
disappear into the floorboards.

She frequents gardens longing
for an encounter with a swarm of bees,
loves to watch them suck a rose to sleep,
drown wildflowers in their narcotic music:
sweet terror buzzing into the sunset.

She no longer fears bugs.
Lies naked on her bed waiting for one
to crawl up her arm to flick
onto the cracked ceiling,
its fragile body unraveling above her.

She no longer fears bugs.
She can squash an ant with the tip
of her tongue, bite a flea off her dog's nose.
She's getting ready for the giant spider
she knows is waiting for her on the outside.

The Gene

Grace draws blood from my arm.
I don't feel a thing as I pump the red
rubber ball she places in my hand.

This is good, she says, the flow
is consistent, as if my blood is grateful
to come out, has a reason to fill the vial.

They will take it to a lab, run tests to see
if I have the gene that will change my life,
one my grandmother who died

of breast cancer may have passed
to my father on a dark night when he lay
in her womb, my embryo dad unaware

he was being nourished by what might
someday kill his daughter.
Are you Ashkenazi? Grace asks me,

like I would know, the needle stuck
in my arm, her question as foreign
as the idea that I could be carrying

a death sentence gene, that my ovaries
might be time bombs
ready to bust my guts in two.

If I have the gene I might die sooner
than Grace unless she dies in an explosion
at a stadium watching baseball or running

in a terminal to catch a plane.
Her hand on my arm, my imagination
bleeds into my mind. If I have this gene

will I remove my breasts just to be safe,
or will I keep them as promises to myself
that something tragic will happen even though

it will anyway, with or without, I am bound to die
as is Grace, as did my father on the golf course
one smoggy day, not a gene that took him,

just his blood stopped flowing, his heart
gave out, the red rubber ball
could no longer pump.

Women's Competition

The Chinese divers are so good
they barely make a splash.

Before they plunge, they arrange
their bathing suits, their cheeks, their hair.

With outstretched arms, legs pointed like birds
swooping down for fish they slice the water

as clean as a knife into angel
food cake, emerging spotless, the diver,

the dive and the water all one, making
it look easy as powdering your nose,

quick and deep as a tetanus shot,
lovers breathing together, synchronized

like watches before the heist,
the water is the music they keep time to,

their own reflections drawing them backward
hands tight behind their knees.

Testing for Acid Reflux

Sandy haired man, blue lab coat
orders her to drink liquid chalk
from a daisy paper cup.
She downs it like a shot,
guzzles another—she can do it, she
can do it—she can swallow
whatever it takes to solve the lump
in her throat mystery,
her throat lit from inside so lab man—
blue veins running through his chalky
hands—can observe the flow
as it travels down her esophagus,
into her stomach, as he lowers the heavy
board she's leaning against, she gulps,
her body reclining so he can study
the journey, excitedly pointing
to the x-ray: *You can see it*
look here—the liquid bubbles back up
like a heart rejecting a memory,
one she might have had while shopping,
cooking, like the time she was late
to pick her boy up or when her father died
before she could see him,
a thought she can't stomach in her head,
a sip that simply refuses to be swallowed.

The Mole They
Cut Out of Your Chest

Where is it now?
Deep, you told me, they had to dig
through the heat to carve it out
this mole, an annoying imperfection

you wanted to be rid of.
Where is it now?
Did they name it before drowning it
in a saline filled test tube, or

did your mole escape?
Could it be traveling through space—
an eye craving new skin to grace,
hoping to land on the inner thigh

of a goddess or the cheek bone
of the girl you once loved?
I always noticed it, was attracted by the way
it glistened, brown, well-defined,

attentive on your smooth chest—
stood out like a special moment,
a warning, a button I might push
to let me inside.

Not having had the chance to say goodbye
I feel sad, missing the spot
that followed me as you'd slide
in and out looking into my eyes

the only flaw on your perfect skin.
Where is it now, the mole they cut out of your chest?
If it gets in touch, please tell it to come
languish behind my ear, ride high

on my shoulder praying to the sun,
or roll on my index finger
waiting for me to blow it away
into the Santa Ana winds.

First E-Mail of the Day

Dawn, before coffee
stranger in my e-mail.
"My Boyfriend's dick keeps slipping out"

Slipping out of what? I'm fuzzy—
his pants, the house, town?
Her boyfriend's dick

keeps slipping out.
Does he know it's missing?
Has his dick left his body,

why must I read this
before the sun is out,
what kind of day will it be?

Now I'm wondering about his dick—
is this a medical condition?
Do others have it—hundreds of dicks

slipping out, wandering off
winding through boulevards
in search of love,

their snakelike selves . . .
I don't know her boyfriend
or his dick, but I'm upset knowing

it keeps slipping out, worried
my boyfriend's dick
is slipping out, wonder

if one day it might wander
into a family's backyard
become King of the worms,

only to be dug up
by their dachshund,
brought home for dinner.

Palm Beach Poetry Festival: First Night

I wake every hour,
as if my child had a fever,
or my cat was about to explode.
I wake, can't remember my name,
why I'm alone, in this hotel.
I'm awakened by titles spilling out
on the pillow, characters walking
through a revolving door: cowboys,
debutants, little people carrying bundles,
dogs in jet skis hurled through windows.
I wake pressing my hand to my chest,
ready to get up but it's the middle
of a harsh night.
I wake looking for someone to race down
to Delray Beach, where the winds are blowing
everyone blind. I'm awakened by the thunderous
night ocean, scent of seaweed, salt, jasmine
seeping through sliding doors
from the balcony where a tipsy chair
rattles against the railing.
I wake anxious for words
to come as fast as a sudden downpour,
so I can lay them on paper like a meal
served to the hungriest guest.
I wake every hour like my grandmother
when I'd sleep over, checking to be sure
I was placed in the middle of the bed,
in the middle of the night when I'd wake

excited to be in this different place,
damp, holding, wanting to ignite
my own *clear expression of mixed feelings*.

Huge Rat in Laundry Room

written on a post-it stuck to the coffee maker
I read it first thing in the morning my son wrote it
the night he came home with his dirty clothes
dumped them in the laundry room
the rat standing in the middle of the floor next to the washer
looked up at him when I saw the post-it at 6 AM
I wondered why he didn't scream when he saw the rat
how did it get in under the cabinets
you know they can shrink down to the thickness
of paper their bones collapsing like years
they can slink in or out of any hole
crawl space sealed corner squeeze themselves like toothpaste
through a hair fracture in cement
I imagine its nose bobbing around my laundry
sniffing panties in the dark
looking up at my son who came home last night
to dump his clothes have a bite to eat
sleep in the bed where he became a man

Lucy

Lucy died from a stroke after she
puked into my old velour shirt,
soaking it with her last bits of table scraps.
Collapsed paws engraving the rug.
We watched her middle of the night
convulsions her round chest harden
she sucked the carpeting into her last breath.
Lucy, fake mother to Beavis our second
brought him home as a puppy
when Lucy was seven.
She taught him to pee on the rosemary bush,
growl at the morning light,
beg for food our son would slide
down his leg into her mouth.
Beavis now spends his days
sniffing for Lucy who's chewing the endless
bone in Chihuahua filled heaven,
signaling Beavis from above, to alert him
a crumb is about to be dropped.
Yesterday I saw Beavis look up at nothing.
But I know it was Lucy beckoning him
into the shadow she left in our back yard.

Alt. Flute 101

This morning I'm grateful for my husband's
snoring: same sounds, always.
One more week 'til our son will swap
blue Pacific for flat Ohio.
I lie in bed, mind racing like the silver scooter

he crisscrossed through Roxbury Park,
feeding him ground turkey, peas thawed in ice trays,
dropping him off first preschool day, Hollywood
backyard I worried had needles in the grass.
"Would you want him to be a baby forever?"

the waxer lady asks, ripping off stray hairs
that want to hang on the way I want my boy to stay?
"Sure," as if I'd give up years of future for one more 2am
feeding, breasts spurting milk as I guzzle apple juice,
and we fall back to sleep, the three of us tucked tight

in damp sheets. *"College is so exciting,"* a friend says,
*"maybe he'll take Alternative Flute, read the classics . . .
In the room the women come and go . . ."* trudging
through Columbus snow. "This is a good time," others say,
"the best years are to come." But what if the best flew by

in a shopping cart, evaporating like the ghost who hid
behind the capes and cowboy hats in the upstairs closet?
Anxious to step into new air, our son circles the edges of his life,
ready for different sounds, as I, grateful for my husband's snoring,
prepare to keep watch over a new life forming once again.

Next Time No Potatoes

I line up the ingredients:
thick cut brisket,
short ribs packed tight,
bay leaves, chicken stock,
fat organic carrots,
a recipe from my secret lover,
this is different stew, he tells me,
this won't taste like any other.
Perhaps he cooked this while his wife,
in the music room, metronome pulsing
Chopin on the grand, aroma of beef
distracting her from playing,
sipped vodka from a flask,
just as I, unsure cook
take a sip of wine
for each splash into the pot,
pondering rice or potatoes,
which will it be?
His notes aren't clear,
why didn't he specify?
One hardly needs two starches,
potatoes or rice, one must
make a choice.
I put them both in,
watch the rice suck up the gravy
like cotton soaking up blood,
as the white bumps of potato
squat in the heavy pot.
At dinner my guests chatter

as they fork potatoes to the sides
of their different colored bowls,
I drift off imagining how I'll tell him
rice is all you need.

Old Man at Trader Joe's

one slice of brie
wrapped in plastic
sitting in the giant
grocery basket
nothing else just
the cheese sitting on top
in the metal cart
the man pushing it
looks lost has forgot
What else do I need?
What else
do I need?
he remembers he needs
nothing but brie
already ripe

Killing the Fly

She knew when it was time for the fly to die.
She knew the moment she was ready
to wave the book in the air haul its tiny body
across the room where she was trying to read herself
to sleep. All tucked in after another day of fighting
traffic eating something over or under cooked
shutting out the singing neighbors, alone
at last in her bed, buzzing, louder and closer until the fly
is practically in her eye. She opens her book:
"He entered the room like a thief, and she was waiting
like the vault he was desperate to crack open . . ." buzz buzz buzz
buzz buzz she tries to ignore it keeps reading but he's fluttering
against her own fluttering lashes he wants to buzz
her head off she's letting him until the second she knows
it's time for the fly to die licks her lips the muscles in her right arm
flex into balls of killing power she slams that fly with everything
she's got watches it sail through the air land inside her blue shoe
with the open toe the one she wore last night when he said what nice shoes
where did you get those like why would he care now the fly
is there, resting in peace inside her shoe where her sole would go
on the floor of the night.

PEOPLE GIVE ME TITLES

The Nudists Are
Getting Ready to Pack

How do the nudists get ready to pack?
Do they pack in the nude
or do they dress to get in the mood?
What will the nudists pack
when the nudists are ready to pack?
Clothes so bare of threads only the nudists
can see them?
Clothes without zippers, buttons or hooks
so the nudists can be nude again soon?
For the nudism curious, some important facts:
Nudism takes place in every corner of the globe.
Nudists have beautiful clothes they never wear
but keep as pets: china red silk blouses,
burlap trousers, angora sweaters, knee high boots
with skinny heels they put on leashes and walk.
Nude areas are isolated from non-nude areas
so encounters with clothed people are less likely:
(*hey, look at the nudists!*)
Our itchy turtlenecks clinging to our throats,
we will never be free of care;
not even the weakest nudist would suffer,
what on earth should I wear?
For nudists, clothing is redundant:
the skin on their bodies is the perfect outfit.
You'll rarely hear a nudist say,
should I pack that extra jacket?

Nightingale Fever

Nightingale Fever doesn't hurt
but you will hiccup until blind
leaving you to see
with other senses
touching elephants
tastes of cherries and mud
the sound of a desperate kiss
helicopters chopping your nights
into fragments of missing person dreams
heat under the table from your dog panting
smells of weeds from childhood baths
shared with your sticky brother
and you will write with eyes closed as the words
slip out like charms from your dead uncle's pocket
Nightingale Fever won't condemn you
to bed but to a sleep of memories
you'll record on the insides of your thighs
birdbath on the crazy neighbor's terrace
your father walking you to school
while spitting in the gutter
the creepy pony you wouldn't get on
sleepover when Rita showed her red hair
you'll write faster thoughts stepping
on each other's faces underneath the covers
poems coming one after another
as you struggle to join what was
to create what might be

Bent Daisies

I see them at the store
stems wrapped in brown paper
green pink blue yellow orange
must be dyed can't be their natural colors
but I'll bring these daisies home they match
everything I will arrange them
green in the blue vase pink in the clear
some by my bed to look at before sleep
daisies—the M & Ms of flowers—
impossible to cry when you see them
they are lemon drops positive flowers
bring good news not complex orchids
plumeria lavender Tiger Lilies
those can *bring you down* beg sadness
daisies are all personality clean simple
generic sweetness no trouble as I take the brown paper off
I am stunned to see my easy-going fun-loving catch a wave
daisies are bent can't stand up straight difficult daisies
I condemn them to the crummy vase
the one up there I can't reach barely give them
enough water to survive this wretched afternoon
but later when I glimpse them falling over spread out splayed
they are dancers praying I carry them back
into the light

Lean into your feelings,

said the life coach,
I read it in the paper
she tells people to lean
into their feelings like
climbing into our dead shadow
catch our feelings off guard
snuggle them suffocate them
push them onto the floor
shove them aside
collide with them—do they know
we're coming after them
whispering into their ears
lean into them, let's
lick them grab them confide clutch hide them
put them up our ass
sit on them hurt them before
they hurt us!
Lean into your feelings:
graze them fondle them know them like a sister
smell them shave them
love them bury them hold them cuddle toss kick them
Lean into your feelings, said the life coach,
be their friend keep them where we can see them
just like our enemy and
pray they fade away like a memory
we never knew we had

His Flavors Are Tender

night time at a gelato cafe she sees him
is attracted by the way his hand
cradles the dish stirred by how he feeds
the sweetness into his mouth closing his eyes
with each spoonful
so distracted she barely touches
her Mexican vanilla mango pistachio melting fast
she imagines him feeding her
she wants to be the plastic spoon he's licking
on both sides his shoulders twitching wants to be inside
the deep cup he's scraping on the bottom she thinks
his flavors are tender as her own lips
she longs to make out with him all night
their flavors mingling as she feeds him her body
one bite at a time

The Teeth Beyond My Window

the teeth beyond my window
are wanted in 50 states
they are bad
cannot be captured
the teeth beyond my window
hover in the cold night
a dangerous mouth
eating out the darkness
grinding themselves into shapeless mounds
so hungry coyotes who dance around them
will not see their anxious white hearts

the teeth beyond my window
rise from my dreams
like heavy fog
angry reflections of my secret sleep mirror
sharp and crooked

this is no life
not for me, not even for these teeth endlessly chattering
like a body shaking out morphine
a chorus line of jagged white tipping their chipped hats
their own private nightmare club
waiting to take a bite out of their next sleeping victim

He Has Nothing Left to Say

He has nothing left to say
Nothing left to say sober
Nothing left to say drunk
Nothing left to say with his clothes on
Nothing left to say naked on the floor

He has nothing left to say
He has said it all
He has said it yelling
He has whispered it into his chest
He has nothing left to say

He has nothing left to say
He has said it to his wife
He has said it to his children
He has said it to strangers in shops
He has said it to his friends
He has said it to those he hasn't cared about in years
He has nothing left to say to those he loves

He has nothing left to say
But he will say it anyway
He will say it loud
He will say it so you can't hear it
He will say it clearly
He will mumble it to the dogs
He has nothing left to say
But he is still speaking
Every day

The things I do in my car

no one knows
the things I do in my car

my traveling L.A. secret circus
cruising around lucky I haven't killed anyone

swerve to the left not looking must
be careful there's something on my leg an itch

someone to my right looking in
you're the only one I'll tell but once I cried

reached under my skirt to feel I was alive
slow roll through the red

not even my therapist can know
the things I do in my car

skin-popping words on my arm
tangerine juice rolling down my thigh

I solved a murder made love to a stranger
fell for a loser wet my eyeliner brush with my tongue

drove my baby to sleep years ago
I'd ride around at dusk waiting for his crying to subside

he screeched as I wound through the canyon
breathing in my future as he'd drift away

his fever dreams melting into Sundays spent
curling down the California incline watched the ocean

follow me north took my dress off cranked up the '60s
blasted the news out of the sunroof flashed

on the subway I used to ride back then stuck inside
suffocating black breezes no secrets no rays hitting me

no top down no windows just darkness grazing
the shoulders of strangers

hoping to get there safe destination 57ᵗʰ street
sticky floating people up on the sidewalk stepping faster

racing the cars hot from exhaust
no ocean just lights red green busses yellow heat

not from sun but bodies
drenched in their own distress

the smell of fumes bouncing off the eastern sky
so low I could catch them in my mouth

not the high western sky where I drive for an endless day
racing the sea where the things I do in my car

only matter to me because no one knows
no one sees

The Woman Who
Mistook a Bug for a Nut

I see her in the garden
sitting in the grass still wet
from morning, spidery weeds

sticking to the soles
of her bare feet, legs crossed
paper plate brimming with salad

juggled on her thighs.
I am mesmerized by the katydid
green as butter lettuce

crawling up her leg
digging into the crispy
romaine. I know it's only

a matter of time
before she'll lift a forkful
into her hungry mouth.

Do I warn her? No.
Do I stop her? Not that either.
She's a stranger yet

I already know too much.
When she bites down onto
the head of the innocent insect,

she closes her eyes savors
what she believes to be a rare nut
from the floor of a rain forest.

Print Wendy's Notes

she is alone in the room
birds abandon trees as
darkness stamps the sky
it's safe to know things
light—guardian of secrets—
protects us from—
she bolts the door
takes a deep sip of dusk
knows she must
print Wendy's notes
wade through the iceberg
compulsion of Wendy's mind
her notes an untrustworthy map
of her secret life
we never forget the moment we choose
to know the truth—have the slap of life
knock us back into
the silence we came from
he told her
if you want to know me, you'll
print Wendy's notes
absorb her confessions
as if they were your own:
Popcorn, apples, peacock feathers,
Remove toe ring, his place at 7,
Count freckles, call M back,
Clean out the dungeon, wash scarves,
Tell him yes, stop remembering,
shampoo Lester,

Count the purple party plates,
Love Wendy forever
she stuffs them in her pocket
burning a hole the size
of the one in her heart
walks through it like a starlet
gliding through a ring of fire
Love Wendy forever: do nothing else
all she wanted was to do just that.

drops on the mirror

she read the note
on the kitchen table
"why are there drops
on the mirror?"

in the bathroom
hundreds of them
some still and solid
in their perfect roundness

tiny open mouths
shiny blisters hugging glass
she looking at them
them looking back at her

some rolling down
drizzling, streaking
like rain on the windshield
had she been watching herself cry?

her eyes two BB guns
shooting tears
hitting the glass now blurry
she knows to never

wipe them away
the drops slowly glide down the glass
like moisture that slides
down the insides of her thighs

she wants to see how far they go
to know how it will end
when there are no more
when all becomes dry

The Runaway Poem

If you see a poem
crawling through your backyard
do not panic

find its trail of lies
watch it
do not coax it to leave

the runaway poem
will only bite you
if you try

to change it, understand it,
or give it
deeper meaning

to capture it
offer it the perfect ending
it will jump into your hand

like a dizzy sparrow
mouth wide open
sucking on the wind

toss it some words:
mushroom lizard, forgotten
tulip, courageous sonata,

it will circle
around you
like an ecstatic puppy

encourage the runaway poem:
lounge on the edge of the page
forget you were ever a poem

stop trying to please make love
to each of your words
do it poem do it!

be aware the runaway poem
may be scared
and searching

for a purpose
a pure voice
it cannot be trusted

if you have reason to believe there's a poem
hiding in your house
do not notify the authorities

there will be paperwork
lines, words crawling
toward you mimicking the poem

poems multiply even
handcuffed, seated in cars
staring out windows

The Door (1)

His side of the door painted
Navajo white—stark, quiet
begging
for clutter

Her side frantic with photos
green and red pushpins colliding
through the years
a lonely dog fur black
with dirt a family wearing goofy beach hats
frozen in chairs by a lake
a mother pushing a stroller smiling big
tiny yellow boots peeking out of a pink blanket
a girl naked in her best yoga pose

The door
separates their rooms
keeps them burning
keeps passion from flying off
keeps them wanting

In her head she begs him
open up let me have a look let me see inside
he doesn't ask
not even
in his head he knows
she would show him more than he could stand
her room so bright color flowers
a window facing the sea her bed
a target

Opening
the door
is their only chance to slam it shut
crushing air

The Door (2)

the door
keeps her safe from herself
room 713, she's added it up
lucky 11 the fancy hotel excites her
twirling her hair warm in the tub
sipping something dizzy
the bar downstairs crawling with ideas
she ponders each one thinks how they
might feel these strangers in soft coats
all arms and hands mouths riding the elevator up
lovers by the time they reach her floor
opening the door which
no longer protects her

The Door (3)

The girl sleeps in her grandmother's bed
down the hall from the kitchen
The door
separates her from all things grown up:
the smell of meat cooking, cigarettes, Chanel
her joke telling uncle, Gretel's stories of bargains, fancy
coats, pretty drinks, shuffling cards, whispering voices
people who know things

She's there as a treat, a getaway, *special*
says her grandmother, the most a six year old
can get at freedom
The girl wakes, struggles to listen
catch a clue why her mother is so sad, but
the door protects her

Alone in bed
still damp from her bath starched white sheets
she rolls over on her stomach
begins to rock
She'd give away her best Barbie
to know the secrets they were telling
stories of her mother who comes home late
or never or with a different stranger
whom she can hear but never see who makes her wish
her bedroom had
a door

When Gifts Go Wrong

What happens when gifts go wrong?
Cashmere socks shoot you looks from inside the box.
Pink lacey top glides off the coffee table suffocates your poodle.
Elegant purse reminds you of your aunt,
Dead by her own hand you were too little to understand
Her husband had a lover, male
Dancer from the Village she took pills kept in her vintage clutch,
What happens when gifts go wrong?
A bicycle too high for her tiny legs they make her get on,
She falls they scream: you bought it she was too small you made her . . .
The booties for the German shepherd—stupid, he says,
Dog hates them she forces them on
Paws lifting like a marching band on fire, what happens
When gifts go wrong?
Cashmere socks so perfect until he uses them to hang himself—
Soft, colorless as wheat, stretched longer than his neck, paler
Than the girl who finds him Christmas morning
Receipt still tight in her hand.

"She Showed Me Pictures of Injuries"

"I met a girl who skates in the roller-derby
she showed me pictures of injuries
lobby of the Hilton
cold in Wisconsin" he tells me
met a girl called Hot Pink Suede
hanging with Jazz Night Queen the two
locked their pretty ankles he saw their bruises
wiped out welts streaked their calves
Hot Pink Giggling inside her drink
she showed him pictures of injuries
he could hear the swelling on her arms
wanted to lift her up into the lobby sky
couldn't get enough of her flying on those skates
tossed across the gym him
braced on the other side
wanting to take the hit full force
her solid smoking body
he closes his eyes sees her flying
she tugs at Jazz Night dizzy their short skirts
singing to him he's cold in Wisconsin he watches them kiss
he met a girl who skates across his face
she licks the cut on Jazz Night's lips
he tastes the blood they laugh Jazz falls off
the lounge onto the checkered carpet smelling of cigarettes
bad teeth battered with footprints from a million skaters
rolling in for a quickie showing pictures of injuries
he wishes he was responsible for

The Coffin Bone

Karen asked me what I thought it means:
The coffin bone

Maybe it means the one part so strong it cannot die
The smooth hard part that stays vibrant forever
hides in our thoughts moves us to tears even in death
Maybe it means the last image we see
in our hungriest nightmare
The murder weapon
The succulent part of the ribs we keep sucking forever
Slang for the best sex we never have or the best sex
after death, the aura around a grave, the way the air
hangs when you look into the face of someone you once
cried for, but then I cheated
I had to know I had to see what the coffin bone really was
coffin bone
n.

The bone enclosed inside a horse's hoof

The one that will never hurt.

CRANKY IN PARADISE

Green Is the New Pink

Happy is the new stupid
Depressed is the new smart
Vodka is the new ice-cream
Gelato is the new sex
Sex is the new heroin
Heroin is the new vacation
Sunset is the new Fountain
Gay is the new straight
Green is the New Pink
Pink is the new black
Death is the new death

She can't work

if the chair is there
she can't think
if the clothes are dirty

she can't visualize
turquoise water in Bermuda
white chickens or what can happen next

if food is sticking
to this morning's dishes
she can't work

if the chair is there
itchy leopard pattern
too large for the space

was an impulse buy
back when furniture was exciting
when a chair

could change her life
she can't work
so she drags it out

from its living room corner
scrapes the hardwood floors
pushes it into the front garden

where it sinks into the soft wet dirt
freshly watered glistening with
half dead peonies

now the chair out there
a trampoline for squirrels
a home for shedding leaves

Cranky in Paradise

she's at their beach house
aqua and peach on all sides
air sweet enough to pour over pancakes

wet life crawling under her
breaking through the mound of hard
sand she built to rest her head

waves striking every few minutes like
contractions before birth
she rubs her belly hands cold

the deck above shaking with fun-lovers
reminds herself this day will end
but she won't know why

it hurt so much why she was lost
as the milky foam
chasing her away from the shore

she feels the beat of conversation
mixed with the rhythm of the sea
what are they saying up there?

closes her eyes deep breath scent of seaweed
she's fading now counts backwards like when
they took her tonsils out or when they took her

baby out when nothing else mattered
but the sound of their own hearts
paradise was nothing more than being alive

Full Moon

Yvonne says the full moon
makes people act different.
She drives an ambulance,

takes people to the hospital
who are in shock, bleeding,
or stricken by the glare of a moon

so cruel it makes them fight
the freezing air with their fists,
throw themselves against her

like Hefty bags filled to the brim,
go mad when they see a yellow line
painted crooked on the crosswalk.

It's the moon makes them,
pulls them further down
from the down they're already at,

into a place even the moon
can't penetrate.
 I've always loved the full moon,

its romance, how it takes over
the sky like a shining platter,
guides me home through rough nights,

slides me into the safe darkness
of sleep, not savage darkness
the people Yvonne knows, the people

who have to scrape their nuts
selves away from the part that wants
to live, who wear the moon

like deranged hats, closing in
on their crowded minds.
The light of *their* moon floods them

wIth distorted shrieks melting
their eardrums: *stay the fuck away* . . .
Yvonne says the full moon

makes people act different,
even when they're already
different enough.

The Things You Hate

You hate when the sun collapses
into the ocean leaving its purple smudge.
You hate buck teeth, grapes with seeds, frozen
windshields, silent rain.
You hate dragging yourself into Monday.
You hate the look in her eyes when you've gone too far.
You hate the flowers that die on your watch.
You hate being stuck with a sadness that settled deep
in your stomach long ago, you hate feeling it struggle
to lift itself out. You hate her for trying to make it right.
You hate kisses unless they send you to the other place
where you can't remember what you hate.
You hate the empty page: that mountain you climb every day.
You hate words that don't behave, answers you don't have,
the ones you do. You hate the story you have to tell,
the plot you want to change, the water you have to drink.
You hate the fear you hold like a swaddled infant.
You hate the night you can't sleep through, the morning
that comes too fast, her never ending softness, the gag
in your mouth. You hate not knowing how it'll end, you hate
that it isn't already over, you hate that it will end at all.
You hate the memory of your father clearing the kitchen table
with the sweep of his hand.
You hate magicians, prayer, crosses and cults.
You hate the love you need, the moon you crave.

it is what it is

It is what it is
Not what it was or will be
Not what it was yesterday
Or tomorrow will be
It is what it is now, look around, see
It is what it is and it never will be
What it was what it could what it absolutely isn't
It's your shoulder hurting when you lift your arm
Your baby crying all night long
It's your mother dying, your father dead,
It's you starting to look like your Uncle Fred
Whose wife Liz reminds you each day on the phone
it is what it is, but you're not alone
We're all in the same boat, don't get me wrong,
It is what it is, just get along
What it is might be better than what it could be
At least your cat's not up in a tree
That's *not* what it is the cat's right here
Sitting by your feet shaking with fear
She can feel you wondering what might happen next
It is what it is now come here, confess
It is what it is, and I'll tell you the rest
We're all here together in *what it is* land
We all know better we all understand
What it is rolls in our pockets like marbles or dice
It is what it is, don't think about it twice.

Turbulence

The pilot announces
the air will be choppy.

I turn to the clouds
scattered like a pattern on sheets

we'll never sleep on.
I think of your body

pressing me into the hotel bed,
your grip exquisitely tight

around my neck.
I lean my head against the hard

airplane window feel the sun
pull me home

as we bump through unstable air,
rocky as a double life.

I pull the seat belt tight,
search for markings of life below

lakes, forests, baseballs rolling
in backyards too far down to see.

I memorize the sleeping faces
of passengers nearby, all of us

up in the air like the way I feel
each time we part.

The lives we're flying over,
the strangers by our sides

are as unknown as the ones we'll find
once we get back home.

Some Things Don't Change

The same sun that pressed her body
into the chaise at sixteen,
still pins her down today keeping her
from what she should be doing.
Same sun burns her now as did then.

Used to be a small concrete space
behind the apartment, she'd fold herself
into a blanket, pillow to soften the ground—
get tan in spite of the dirty city summer,
imagining herself at the ocean, too much trouble

to get to. Today on the perfect beach
she finds her spot, stretches out like a paralyzed
ballerina, falls into the warmth
holding her in place. At no other time
does she feel like she's moving when she's not, or

can she feel a fire starting inside her—except
when he touches her or whispers things
he wants to do—things the sun can also do.
Heat addict, she craves whatever can change
the colors inside her.

She Knows Where the Milk Is

She knows where the milk is
But cannot find the fridge
Smiles when the moon comes out
She's a champ at solo bridge

She knows how to stir the soup
Recalls how hard it is to love
Is glad her neighbors are peeking in
Spend hours in the tub

She knocks around her house at night
Looking for new games to try
She chases worms in the garden
Wishes her dog could fly

If you see her on the street
Blow a kiss in her direction
She'll be wearing only shoes and socks
Staring at her own reflection

He Doesn't, She Does

He doesn't want to think of her.
Can't risk her face showing up
in his sock drawer,

her butt filling his mind as
salad is served.
He doesn't want to remember

his face between her legs,
a word she whispered on the phone,
can't risk going to sleep imagining

holding her body tucked inside his,
her belly flat under his hand, his mouth
resting against her neck.

He can't think of her when she's not there
only in the moment when and where
they touch they know what might never be,

even then he doesn't want to look; but she
always seems to think of him,
in the shower, in the gym, feels him floating

under the covers while she's tight in bed,
turns into the pillow to crush her head.
She refuses to toss him out of her dreams,

her body aching because it seems
the chance to have him is deliciously slim.
He doesn't think of her; she thinks of him.

She blew her nose

into a fresh pink tee shirt
plucked from her bottom
drawer. It's not that she didn't

have a tissue. She did.
The box on her bedside table
was well within reach

but she preferred the comfort
of cotton, of what she'd worn
the day before

things fell apart. It's safer to cry
into a tissue that can be flushed
in the toilet where she'd

vomited after listening to him
confess, pesto pasta from lunch
fighting its way back up.

She cried until a blue bird
flew out of her body,
the breeze from its wings

making her sneeze.
She blew her nose
into a fresh pink tee shirt

then used it to clean
the things on his bedside
table, rub the alarm

out of his clock, shine
the oval mirror as she watched
her face disappear.

Cloud Coverage on Easter

thick silent dampness
cements the sky
clouds have taken over the universe

breezes are the work
of birds
flapping their wings

struggling to escape
their endless opaque prison
the sky their playground

today their enemy
threatens to explode its whiteness
into tinted air

we on the ground
want nothing
but to be indoors

removed from this monotonous
blank canvas no color heaven
we squint from below

calling for sun wishing
for planes beckoning birds
to break up the boredom

cloud coverage on Easter
is why we're not
at the ocean where sometimes it's blue

like the eggs we dip
dye staining white towel
white as the sky that keeps us in

Waiting for You in the Bar

I'm here you're
here, but we're here
separately, you in the room
flooded with smoke and sun

me in the lounge dark leather
seats surrounded by darker light.
I think you're not coming
forgot or got stuck in the endless

traffic we now call home.
I drink a tall vodka, suck the straw,
my only chance to survive,
get it deep inside, shut down the thought

you might not be arriving.
I know you're here, can feel you,
you're never late,
you don't forget, but I can't get

myself to look around, rather
drink another, imagine strolling
onto the beach, tide rolling out
wandering into someone else's dream,

a kiss floating onto my lips, maybe
yours? A white bird hovering
sending signals from a forgotten planet
calling me into another life.

I'm here, you're here, but it doesn't matter:
we've already been there and gone,
the moon following until it's ready
to pull us back.

I Am Returning

I return the shoes
Because they do not fit
I wanted them to fit so I
Pretended they fit in the store
But they don't fit
The black shoes

I return the dresses
I bought for my mother
She doesn't like them
She wanted to like them but she
Doesn't like them
The cotton print dresses

I return the meatballs
Because they taste bad
I was excited to eat them
But now I am convinced
They will kill me
The four turkey meatballs

I return the spiders
Outside to scatter
Into the dark moist corners of the night
Hatch their sticky green eggs
Take over the earth
The dark brown spiders

I return the lipstick
I stole from Walgreens
It is not my color
Though I'd hoped it might be
Besides, the guilt is killing me
The light pink lipstick.

The Necessary Orange

She carries it in her purse
Takes it out
When she's ready

Balances it on her lap
Peels slowly
Inhaling citrus sticking

To her yellow skirt
Glowing with white polkadots
This is her 11 AM snack

Alone on the park bench
The orange is her company
Separates each section

Imagining where she'll go
This summer on vacation
The beach in California or a city

She's never seen
Wherever she decides
She will have an orange

in her purse
To take out and savor
When the moment moves her

3 AM

middle of the night, middle of her life
she opens her eyes, one lash at a time
a song sings through her, a memory
her shoulders stones from the bottom of a river
one second until darkness takes her back to sleep

How To

How to Relax

Sit back,
look down,
imagine your lap
a stage filled with dancers,
toes pointing up,
your face their target
Deep breath in
out on three, now
imagine your lap
a lake filled with spotted
fish floating backward,
a starlet on the shore
toes in the water.
Keep focused:
Imagine your lap
the abandoned nest
of a loon
lost in the wrong
hemisphere
diving for fish
floating backward
in the lake
your lap used to be.

How to Talk to Water

Be brief.
Don't use big words.
Go with the flow
but be concise.

When talking to a lake,
stream, river, or into
a puddle, it's okay
to smile at your

reflection. Go ahead,
wink. Say it all:
You're sick of your life,
you're tired of struggling.

You're not ready
to give up, but damn it,
you're ready
for something new.

The water is there for you.
If you're disgusted
go ahead, spit.
Watch it dissolve.

Be aware,
talking to the ocean
is more complex.
You must use sprawling

gestures or the ocean
will not recognize you.
Be advised:
do not wear a wetsuit

or the ocean will laugh.
Never spit in the ocean.
For best results,
whisper into the surf

until the cold foam curls
around your ankles.
Then you will know
you have been heard.

How to Eat Turkey
if You Don't Like Turkey

Don't look at it while you eat.
Look across the table and watch the lips
of others. Wonder what they taste like.

Tear off bite-sized pieces
with violent snaps,
feel the meat in your fingers

while imagining the skin
of a stranger, dark hair
just before you enter.

Dip into gravy thick and rich
as your fantasies, murky
as the New York Thanksgiving sky.

Gently place the turkey in your mouth,
feel the juices
drench your tongue,

pretend chewing it will save your life.
Close your eyes when you swallow
so your hosts will believe it tastes good.

Let it drip, just a drop,
onto your pants stretched
with expectations.

How to eat turkey
if you don't like turkey?
Think about what you do like:

the hardest slap when you're not prepared,
the softest kiss when you are, your face
trapped inside your lover's dream.

How to Look at Clouds

Look up and watch them pass.
You will see
how meaning can form

out of nothing.
Often they go too fast:
A ghost drains into a building,

sheet of light is torn
by an impatient breeze
disappearing into the hilltops.

Go to the beach during a storm.
Look up and watch them gather,
one explosive bruise

after another,
forcing themselves
into the mouth of the sea.

Walk through the park
on a humid day.
Look up watch them collect,

bulky cotton cumulus,
thunderheads guarding
the troubled sky.

You may find today
there are no clouds.
You have looked up many times

see nothing except
endless blue
warning you that nothing

will change.
I say clouds are where
you find them.

One might be stuck
at the edge
of a mountain range so far

you can almost feel
the chill from the air
that surrounds it.

Do not obsess about
any one cloud.
They are passing

for your wonder.
They will only form
in that moment

you are ready to be
convinced.
Chances are there's a cloud

whispering your name
into the ear of a sideways bird
carrying a message to God.

How to Celebrate Your Birthday

Wake up ready to evacuate.
Toss everything out of your bed:
bullets, razors, long
extension cord, keep only the soft
woman stretched out for you to see.
Re-evaluate the symbols on your walls,
pudding boiling on the stove,
midgets in your bread drawer.
Birthdays are serious.
Make a list of what is no longer useful:
bean bag chair, thank you notes, ice trays.
Set them all on fire while you stare into yourself,
one year older ready for a laugh.
Who cares about hilltops stabbing a sky
so blue it hurts to see? Who cares
about granite counters built-in
jacuzzis? It's your birthday so jump the wall
fall into the arms of the only one who can
catch you: watch her smile when you land.
Spread the icing from your cake
over her ready shoulders,
lick it off while she watches the candles burn
down into the center of chocolate.

How to Have a Nice Day

Sit on the porch in a wicker chair,
any porch you find with flower pots
crawling with color you can kick over:
watch the dirt settle in the cracks.
Sit up straight, meditation style,
look to your right, left,
imagine yourself on the swings
of your past, take a deep in,
out, expel one thought under your breath,
too awful to say out loud
one you've saved in secret,
about your mother or significant
other, the thought you savor, like a ripe
raspberry floating in your cereal.
Have a nice day.
Have the kind of day
you'll dream about tonight,
filled with twisted chitchat,
three changes of clothing,
men, women kissing your feet,
bringing you platters of fruit,
a day bursting with promise,
ideas, a white cat spotted in the alley,
a lost love letter found in your grey jacket pocket.
How to have a nice day?
Let it all go: wild eyebrows, poached
egg, hospital corners, sand in your shoes.
Get on your knees and check under the bed
for clues about who you are. You will find a folded

body, yours years younger, someone
to confide in, pull apart, throw into the next
nice, treacherous day.

Air Kissing on Mars

Extra-terrestrial kisses
ricochet off soft cheeks
of space debutantes, flooding
pink air, bubbles
at a toddler's birthday.

Where there's life there's air
kissing especially on the feverish
red planet where deep kissing
is outlawed except behind
the pedestal craters of Utopia.

You see stray air kisses
vanish in endless sand storms
breathless, lone journeying
to forbidden galaxies,
floating through freezing temperatures,

half told stories, open wounds
between two moons, ambushed by Martian
police, hidden in soil samples
waiting to be released as prizes
to the first humans who touch down safely.

Biographical Note

Kim (Freilich) Dower grew up in New York on the Upper West Side of Manhattan and received a BFA in Creative Writing from Emerson College in Boston.

Upon graduating, Kim stayed at Emerson where she taught Introduction to Creative Writing: Poetry for two years before moving to Los Angeles where she pursued other writing projects and began her own literary publicity company called Kim-from-L.A., the name for which she has become famous in the world of book publishing.

A few years ago, "like magic, like a dream," poetry re-entered her life and the poems have been rushing out as if a 25 year dam had broken, and she's been writing three or more poems a week.

Kim's work has appeared in *Ploughshares*, *The Seneca Review*, and in the on-line video magazine, *Guerilla Reads*.

She lives with her family in West Hollywood, California.